Original title:
Underneath the Oak's Arms

Copyright © 2025 Creative Arts Management OÜ
All rights reserved.

Author: Seraphina Caldwell
ISBN HARDBACK: 978-1-80567-269-2
ISBN PAPERBACK: 978-1-80567-568-6

A Reverent Pause Beneath the Green

Squirrels dancing on branches high,
With acorns falling from the sky.
A chipmunk juggles, not too wise,
As birds debate who takes the prize.

A picnic spread, ants on parade,
A fruit cup now a fond charade.
Giggling whispers in between,
Nature's laughter, a joyful scene.

The Hidden Paths of Ancient Roots

A rabbit hops, then trips and falls,
A frog croaks jokes, as laughter calls.
The path's a maze, with twists and turns,
Where every step ignites our yearns.

A gnome misplaced his favorite hat,
The toadstools chuckle, 'What of that?'
In every nook, a giggle waits,
Life's little quirks are truly great.

Together in Nature's Embrace

We sing with crickets, night's sweet choir,
While fireflies flicker with mischief's fire.
A raccoon steals snacks, oh what a sight,
While owls hoot softly, 'You're doing it right!'

Beneath the leaves, we find our play,
As laughter weaves through dusk till day.
In every shadow, a joke unfurls,
Nature's humor, a gift to the world.

A Nest of Solitude and Wonder

In a cozy nook, I find my seat,
Where squirrels debate and birds retweet.
A world of chuckles wrapped in foliage,
Nature's comedy, a witty collage.

Bees on a mission, buzzing with flair,
Trying to dance in the sunlit air.
Whispers of leaves, a secret exchange,
The antics of critters — utterly strange!

Nature's Embrace in Green and Brown

A vine that tickles, a trunk that hugs,
While worms wiggle their wiggly plugs.
Beneath the branches, mischief brews,
With a raccoon stealing my favorite shoe!

Grasshoppers jumping like they own the day,
Chirping their tunes, come what may.
Meanwhile, a snail yells, 'I'm almost there!'
But everyone knows he's going nowhere!

Shadows Cast by the Heartbeat of the Earth

In the thick shadows, where giggles roam,
A toad croaks loudly, claiming his home.
Frogs in tuxedos, throwing a ball,
While snails slide by, looking to crawl.

Critters converge for an audacious feast,
An ant-sized drop of jam that was deemed a feast.
They dance and twirl, a raucous delight,
Under the canopy, as day turns to night.

The Haven of Endless Seasons

Autumn leaves tumble, a colorful show,
While chipmunks hoard acorns, all in a row.
Winter wraps in a frosty embrace,
But a raccoon in snow boots? What a sight in this place!

With spring's flowers giggling to bloom,
And summer's sun making room for a groom.
A squirrel in shades, lounging with flair,
Life's a comedy — a wild, joyful affair!

Secrets Wrapped in Bark

A squirrel plotted with acorns bright,
Telling tales from morn till night.
The trees all giggled, roots in a twist,
As secrets spilled that none could resist.

Chirping birds shared the juiciest news,
While bugs danced around in their weekend shoes.
The wind whispered softly, "What's that you say?"
Dancing leaves made it a cabaret!

Shelter from the Blazing Sun

Frogs in sunglasses, lounging about,
Croaking tunes that made all shout.
The rabbits played cards with a sly little grin,
While the sun made shadows where laughter begins.

A turtle saw fit to join in the fun,
Rolling dice with a wink, 'I've yet to run!'
The old crow cawed, in a funny, loud tone,
'Why so serious? Just play and get thrown!'

The Sanctuary of Twisted Branches

Beneath the branches, a party unfolds,
With dancing bugs and stories retold.
A raccoon in a top hat, so dapper and neat,
Juggled wild berries for a lunchtime treat.

The whispers of leaves, like giggles too close,
Join in the fun, laughter's the dose.
While wise old owls chuckle and stare,
At the antics of friends without a care.

Echoes of the Forest Floor

On the forest floor, where all creatures play,
Rabbits and foxes have nothing to say.
They're too busy baking a pie with flair,
While a hedgehog in bow ties hops without a care.

A badger brings snacks, served in a hat,
While a family of ducks sing songs 'round the mat.
With echoes of laughter that flutter like wings,
The forest is buzzing with the joy that it brings.

A Tapestry of Light and Shade

The squirrel's acorn stash is great,
Yet somehow it always seems too late.
He hops around, looking quite absurd,
Wants to beat the jays, but he's not heard.

The dancing shadows twist and twine,
While birds debate if it's snack or dine.
Mistakes abound, they flit and fly,
Oh, what a show beneath the sky!

A rabbit giggles at the fuss,
Hoping no one notices his bus.
Each leap a bounce, each hop a cheer,
He knows it's fun when everyone's near.

The Haven of Leafy Embrace

A picnic spread with care and haste,
Yet ants arrived and joined the feast, they paced.
Honey spills on the checkered cloth,
While someone's sandwich goes and froths.

The wind comes laughing through the boughs,
Making funny faces, as it bows.
A bird drops snacks, a glorious mess,
We wonder how the tree feels, no less!

Some kids are shouting, 'Look up high!'
A plump raccoon steals a peach pie.
Laughter erupts in the shade's thrall,
Beneath the leaves, we're having a ball!

In the Cradle of Old Growth

The old gnarled roots twist like old folks,
Whispering secrets of giddy jokes.
A laughing lizard struts with flair,
Frogs join in, a croaking affair!

Under branches large and wide,
A family of rabbits, huddled beside.
They munch and crunch quite happily,
Sharing tales of grass integrity!

A kid's hat flies with a springy breeze,
While squirrels exchange their nutty keys.
The antics roll, an autumnal play,
What a joy this charming ballet!

Beneath the Verdant Veil

In the shade, a sleepy dog sprawls,
Dreaming of chasing the garden balls.
It's a warm nook, where snores are loud,
He'll wake for snacks, but that's allowed!

A pair of turtles take their cue,
Slow pace in life, like they always do.
Snickering at the rushing group,
They know that fun ain't just a hoop!

Children giggle in whispers faint,
While someone's shoelace might just paint.
Laughter bubbles, like champagne's fizz,
In this green haven, what bliss it is!

Beneath the Canopy of Time

Squirrels giggle as they leap,
Chasing dreams while children sleep.
Beneath the leaves that twist and bend,
Time's a prankster, not a friend.

The whispers of a hidden joke,
As breezes tease the sturdy oak.
Each branch a tale, a giggling sprout,
Where laughter bounces in and out.

In the Shadow of Ancient Boughs

Beneath great limbs, the shadows dance,
Mice in top hats in a trance.
A fox with glasses reads a tome,
While birds play chess and call it home.

The grass grows thick with laughter's sound,
As ants march proudly on the ground.
An old crow caws a comedy,
With punchlines sharp as can they be?

Whispering Leaves and Secrets Shared

The leaves are gossiping today,
Telling tales of a cat's ballet.
A hedgehog winks, he knows the score,
While turtles race—they're slow, not sore.

The breeze plays tricks, a riddle spun,
A game of tag in the warm sun.
With every rustle, giggles grow,
In a secret world, the critters know.

Embrace of the Timeless Tree

In twisted knots, the stories weave,
A bear who's much too shy to leave.
An owl who's wise, but can't do math,
Counts to ten, then takes a bath.

The old bark creaks, a hearty laugh,
As squirrels argue—who's cuter half?
They'll never agree, not on this day,
In the embrace where mischief plays.

Shadows of the Timeless Tree

In the shade where squirrels play,
Laughter bounces day by day.
Chasing acorns, light as air,
How they dance without a care.

Branches whisper, secrets shared,
While raccoons plot, slightly scared.
A critter feast, they're in delight,
As shadows stretch into the night.

Solace in the Gnarled Roots

Gnarled roots wave like crazy hands,
Tickling toes of all who stand.
A cheeky breeze, it lifts our hats,
While nearby squirrels bicker like brats.

Beneath the twists, we find a place,
Where silly dreams embrace our space.
Nature's whimsy, on display,
Invites us all to laugh and play.

Beneath the Boughs of Refuge

Boughs so broad, like a cozy quilt,
Where giggles grow and worries wilt.
Beneath the leafy, green embrace,
A tickle from a bug can chase.

In this nook of tangled glee,
Birds trade tales, wild and free.
With each rustle, a new joke told,
While ants march by, both brave and bold.

Embracing Nature's Guardians

Guardians tall with limbs so wide,
Catching dreams as they glide.
A lizard's dance, an awkward jig,
Fills the air, both sweet and big.

In their shade, our laughter grows,
With every gust, a breeze that blows.
The guardians grin, they join the play,
As sunlight laughs and melts away.

Cradled in Nature's Arms

In a tree, a squirrel did dance,
With acorns that sparkled like a chance.
He twirled and jumped, oh what a sight,
While birds laughed on, taking flight.

A chipmunk stashed snacks with such flair,
He hid them all, without a care.
But forgot where, oh what a shame,
He's now just playing a nutty game.

The sun peeked through with a wink,
Making shadows swirl and blink.
Nature giggled, soft and sweet,
As critters danced on tiny feet.

In this grove, laughter sprouted,
With every rustle, joy was touted.
From twirling leaves to playful barks,
It's a comedy with hidden sparks.

The Cloak of Time in Leafy Shades

Worn leaves whisper grand old tales,
Of squirrels who conquered and woven trails.
Time's cloak wrapped round in leafy dress,
As if nature played, with playful press.

The branches swayed like a silly joke,
While shadows giggled, giving a poke.
Sunshine chuckled, warming the ground,
In this merry wood, joy knows no bound.

Each rustling leaf wore a grin,
As breezes chimed with laughter within.
Memories echoed from years gone by,
In gentle waves, they danced on high.

Oh, the tales the trees could share,
Of playful ghosts that flutter through air.
Time may hide, but it can't suppress,
The merry stories of nature's jest.

Moments Spun in Timber Tales

In a hollow, a raccoon made a home,
With trinkets and treasures from everywhere he'd roam.
He'd tap on wood with his tiny claws,
Painting laughter that nature saw.

The owls at night wore spectacles grand,
Holding secret meetings they'd carefully planned.
They'd hoot about nonsense that only they knew,
While rabbits would giggle, in moonlight's hue.

The squirrels threw acorns like tiny balls,
Creating games with laughter that calls.
A dance party sparked on the grassy floor,
Where even the shadows joined in for more.

Tales spun around in circles and sways,
Celebrating the joy in funny ways.
In each branch, the spirits would waddle,
As moments danced in this wooded coddle.

Harmony Beneath the Wooded Whisper

Beneath the sway of branches wide,
The critters joined for a jocular ride.
With a bunny that sang off-key,
And a turtle who claimed he was free.

The breeze piped in, a comical tune,
As the woodland creatures danced under the moon.
Squirrels twirled, and raccoons chimed,
Laughter echoed through the trees, unconfined.

A deer pranced in with a top hat bold,
Claiming it was the sight to behold.
The fox then dashed, trying to run,
But tripped on vines; oh, what fun!

Harmony rang in this gentle sphere,
Where funny antics filled the air.
In every nook, joy took its flight,
Beneath the whispers of the twilight.

Harmony Wrapped in Nature's Green

The squirrels had a flair for dance,
Chasing shadows, lost in chance.
They twirled and leaped without a care,
In the sun-drenched warmth of air.

The rabbits joined with gleeful hops,
While frogs belted out five-star pops.
A dance-off started in the glade,
As nature's revelry paraded.

The birds, not wanting to be shy,
Joined in chorus, oh my, oh my!
With flapping wings, they stuck around,
Their silly antics knew no bound.

As evening fell, the laughter soared,
Under trees where friendships roared.
In harmony, all beings sang,
Wrapped in joy, the forest rang.

The Lullaby of Leafy Canopies

The leaves laughed softly in the breeze,
Whispering secrets, which brought me ease.
A chubby chipmunk snored with glee,
Dreaming of nuts and an endless spree.

Around him gathered quite the crew,
With crickets chirping a tune or two.
They sang to the moon, so big and bright,
While owls chuckled at the silly sight.

A raccoon slid down the trunk with flair,
Fell on his back, without a care.
The laughter echoed through the night,
As shadows danced in pure delight.

In canopy snug, the night was light,
Nature's humor shining bright.
From all the chuckles emerged a balm,
Creating a world, so sweet and calm.

Sheltering Souls in Nature's Arms

The grass was soft, the sun so bright,
The squirrels claimed it their delight.
In a sleepy grove, they built a nest,
A cozy spot, they felt the best.

A turtle crept in slow parade,
Weaving jokes, a real charade.
With each step, he'd trip in style,
Leaving the crowd in giddy smiles.

An ant with shades strutted by,
Claiming he flew in the sunny sky.
The stories spun in merry cheer,
In nature's arms, there's nothing to fear.

As shadows danced, all creatures near,
Shared a laugh, while sipping cheer.
In this realm of joy so grand,
United we stand, hand in hand.

Embracing the Oak's Whispering Heart

Old Oak stood tall with a witty grin,
Listening close to the fun within.
A family of owls hooted loud,
As squirrels performed before the crowd.

Beneath the branches, shadows played,
With laughter bright, no care betrayed.
A deer tripped over her own two feet,
And landed softly, quite the feat.

The wind piped up, a playful tune,
As blossoms swayed beneath the moon.
With nature's orchestra in full swing,
Every creature joined to laugh and sing.

So here we gather, wild and free,
In this haven of humor and jubilee.
With every chuckle and joyful spark,
We dance together in the old oak park.

Serenity Wrapped in Verdant Hues

In the shade, the rabbits race,
While squirrels plot and keep their pace.
A dog dressed up in summer gear,
Chases bees, but won't come near.

The sun drips gold on grassy blades,
Where tiny ants make grand parades.
The gopher grins with muddy paws,
While birds debate world's quirkiest laws.

A picnic spread, a splash of jam,
A sneaky raccoon plotting a scam.
Laughter echoes through trees so wide,
Where even nature joins the ride.

With laughter loud, we swing and twirl,
As bees conspire to steal our pearl.
In this green haven, we let loose,
With every giggle, nature's muse.

In the Heart of the Forested Sanctuary

A porcupine with spiky hair,
Winks at us like he just don't care.
Frogs in bow ties croak their tunes,
While owls try their hand at cartoons.

The sun peeks through in funny spots,
Creating shadows, tying knots.
Woodpeckers wear their best attire,
As we dance around the campfire.

With marshmallows set to take a dive,
And chipmunks plotting their surprise.
A turtle moves at snail's own pace,
While laughter fills this joyful space.

A squirrel with acorns, quite the hoard,
Laughs at us while we play the fool.
Nature's jesters in this grand display,
In this leafy stage, we choose to play.

Beneath the Whispering Leaves

A chipmunk juggles tiny nuts,
While a raccoon steals away our guts.
In this green realm, absurdity flows,
As wind plays tricks, and laughter grows.

Beneath a sky that's all but sane,
We dance with shadows, forget the rain.
The sun a spotlight, the breeze our song,
In this forest where we all belong.

A bear in the distance does a jig,
At the sight of his friend, a startled pig.
Together they waltz through ferns and grass,
Nature's comedy - let the moments pass.

Under bright skies, mischief abounds,
With every giggle, joy surrounds.
In hidden glades where the wild things play,
We laugh until the close of day.

Embrace of the Ancient Canopy

A sloth lounges high, taking a snooze,
While raccoons plot to steal our shoes.
The breeze whispers secrets, oh so sly,
As squirrels make jokes that make us cry.

In this realm of mischief and cheer,
Birds wear spectacles, a sight so dear.
A fox tells tales that twist and bend,
While owls hoot warnings without end.

Marshmallows roast with a twist of fate,
As ants begin their dinner plate.
We watch as nature throws a bash,
With every chuckle, there's a splash.

So come along, join the playful spree,
In a world where all wild things are free.
With laughter echoing through the trees,
We find delight in nature's tease.

Dreams Weave Amongst the Twisting Limbs

In the shade, squirrels plot,
Wearing tiny hats and boots.
They conspire, oh so sly,
To steal our picnic fruits.

The sunbeams dance and play,
As bumblebees buzz by,
They laugh at our mishaps,
With a whimsical, 'Oh my!'

A raccoon with a grin,
Winks as he swipes a chip,
With a flourish of his paw,
He performs a little flip.

Oh, the mischief we find,
Amidst the branches sway,
Nature hosts a comedy,
In its own, peculiar way.

The Echo of Leaves in the Wind

Leaves giggle in the breeze,
Whispers of tales untold.
They gossip about the birds,
And squirrels who are bold.

A gust plays tag with twigs,
Tumbling all around us.
One branch, in a silly dance,
Invites the others to fuss.

The crickets join the laugh,
With their chirps on repeat,
A melody of mischief,
Composing quite the beat.

And when the night falls down,
The moon grins from above,
Shining on all the fun,
A night of twinkling love.

Stories Woven in Whispered Breezes

A breeze swirls with a twist,
Tickling every leaf and shoe.
It carries tales of jest,
Of hedgehogs with a view.

The butterflies all flutter,
In a dance that's quite absurd,
As they plot a silly scheme,
To hide from the fluttering herd.

An owl hoots with delight,
As rabbits chase their tails,
While toadstools share the giggles,
In tiny, merry trails.

The woods become a stage,
For laughter and for cheer,
In this delightful realm,
We're free to shed a tear.

Guardians of the Woodland Realm

The wise old tree stands tall,
Guarding secrets and fun,
With branches reaching wide,
In prankster ways, they run.

Chipmunks dress up as knights,
With acorn caps held tight,
They joust on mossy ground,
In their playful, furry plight.

A fox with a sly grin,
Counts the stars with a plot,
He's dreaming up his scheme,
To sneak the snacks we've got.

And though the woodland plays,
In antics of pure glee,
These guardians of the land,
Ensure our smile's a key.

Beneath the Wise Old Branches

In a haven where squirrels plot and play,
An acorn party starts at break of day.
The branches sway with laughter tight,
As birds perform their morning flight.

A raccoon spills tea, what a comical sight,
While a curious fox takes a nap in the light.
Leaves rustle jokes like a whispering breeze,
Nature's stand-up, putting minds at ease.

A hidden gnome grins beneath a cloak,
With mushrooms as chairs, what a hoax!
Frogs leap in rhythm, frogs jump and croak,
In this woodland world, laughter's bespoke.

From roots to treetops, silly things thrive,
A dragonfly's waltz keeps the mood alive.
So join the fun, like a leaf that flutters,
In this sanctuary where giggles are uttered.

The Shelter of Nature's Guardians

In a circle where shadows play tricks,
A snail on a skateboard does flips.
The owls chuckle with wise, knowing eyes,
While the bumblebees hum their hilarious lies.

Beneath the stout limbs, a mouse tells a tale,
Of cheese he once saw that was larger than a whale.
The laughter erupts, a joyful spree,
As the sunbeams join in, bright and free.

A hedgehog strolls in with flair and grace,
Sporting a hat, oh what a face!
The rabbits in wigs prance and bounce,
In this quirky realm where rhymes do pounce.

From dusk till dawn, the fun won't cease,
Among trees standing strong, there's joy and peace.
Nature's guardians guard laughter's embrace,
In this whimsical shelter, find your place.

Cradled by the Gnarled Roots

At the base of the mighty, the giggles arise,
With ants on a train, a sight for sore eyes.
The grasshoppers disco, all scaly and green,
While worms do the worm in this goofy scene.

With roots that twist like contortionist dreams,
A silly old turtle is bursting at the seams.
He tells of the time he raced a swift flash,
But ended up rabbit-lapping with a dash.

A family of mice put on a grand play,
With scripts made of crumbs, they feast all day.
Their stagecloth is silk of the finest soft grass,
Cheese wheels for props—oh, such a fine class!

In this cradle of humor, it's hard not to smile,
Where creatures concoct fun in a delightful style.
The gnarled old roots just embrace the jest,
In a nature-wide giggle, we're all truly blessed.

Where Sunlight Dances with Shade

In a ballet of beams where the shadows prance,
A chipmunk in shades takes a summer's chance.
He glides with a grace that's endlessly funny,
While the flowers bloom proudly in shades of sunny.

The shadows chase sunbeams in playful pursuit,
As a butterfly models a dazzling suit.
They twirl and they wiggle, a silly parade,
In this vibrant arena where laughter won't fade.

A ladybug spots a hippo on a bike,
And giggles erupt as the sun starts to hike.
The breeze carries whispers, tickles the trees,
With the joy of the moment, life flows with ease.

So come share the fun where the light loves to play,
In this garden of glee, time dances away.
Where sunlight and shade write a tale so grand,
Laughter and nature, hand in hand.

A Dialog with the Living Bark

I asked a tree if it could talk,
It said, "Only when you walk!"
I chuckled back, "What do you say?"
"Try to keep the squirrels at bay!"

The roots, they whispered tales of old,
Of acorns dropped and secrets told.
"Did you see the owl's silly dance?"
"Only when he thought he'd prance!"

A squirrel chimed in, "Hey, what about me?"
"You're just the nutty one, can't you see?"
The tree just laughed and swayed a bit,
While we all tried to make a wit!

So here we stand, the wise and spry,
With leafy dreams and jokes that fly.
The bark will giggle, roots will hum,
In this wild grove, we're all quite fun!

The Stillness in a Leafy Passage

In a shade so cool where whispers dwell,
I spied a beetle with tales to tell.
"What's your secret?" I leaned to hear,
He grinned and said, "Stay away from beer!"

A squirrel leapt by with a floppy hat,
"I'm on a mission!" he said, quite fat.
"What's your goal?" I asked with glee,
"To collect all the acorns, just wait and see!"

Leaves rustled high, a breeze so light,
A ladybug danced, oh what a sight!
"Why do you twirl?" I shouted loud,
"I'm waiting for dinner, want to make a crowd!"

In this leafy passage, laughter sings,
With beetles, squirrels, and all those things.
Nature's party, come join the beat,
In stillness we find our funny feet!

Cries and Dreams in the Woodland

Beneath the boughs where shadows play,
I heard a frog shout, "Hip-hip-hooray!"
I asked, "What's the fuss, what's the cheer?"
"Just dropped my lunch; now I want a beer!"

A rabbit rushed past in a sudden dash,
"I'm late, I'm late, oh what a clash!"
"Late for what?" I called with glee,
"To nibble on snacks with a wise old bee!"

The tree declared, "Let's all unwind,
Life's too short to be so confined!"
A chipmunk added, with a cheeky grin,
"Scratch my back, and I'll let you in!"

Cries and dreams, a woodland jam,
Where laughter flows like a well-fed lamb.
Join the merry band, have some fun,
In nature, the giggles have just begun!

A Union with the Earth's Heart

In our hearts we feel the beat,
Pitter-patter, oh what a treat!
The moles dug deeper for a chat,
"Did you hear the one about the fat cat?"

The wind joined in, a gentle breeze,
"I tickle the leaves; it's a breeze to please!"
A worm popped up, with a grand smile,
"How's about we dance for a while?"

A raccoon strolled by with a tiny drum,
"Let's make some music, come on, let's hum!"
With roots all tangled and branches wide,
We're one big family, full of pride!

In this union, where laughter starts,
We celebrate life with open hearts.
The earth shall giggle, the sky shall chime,
Together we dance, no need for a rhyme!

Sentinels of Solitude and Serenity

Two squirrels debate the best nuts,
While a sleepy owl just hoots and struts.
The breeze carries tales, both silly and grand,
As branches sway like a dance at hand.

A rabbit hops in, sporting a hat,
Claiming he's king, oh imagine that!
The shadows giggle at their little spree,
In this leafy realm, they all feel so free.

A woodpecker joins with a rhythm so fine,
He taps a beat on a trunk, so divine.
The sun peeks through, casting such cheer,
In this tree playground, there's joy far and near.

The ground squirrels plot a nutty surprise,
With acorns galore, oh what a prize!
Leaves rustle softly, laughter abounds,
In this quirky haven, happiness sounds.

Soulful Moments Amidst the Canopy

In the shade where the critters convene,
A hedgehog reads gossip, quite the scene.
As ants march by with a picnic feast,
They argue who brings the best kale beast.

A raccoon recites poems, dramatic and bold,
His audience laughs, the tales never old.
Butterflies flutter, wearing a grin,
As bees buzz along, joining in on the din.

A snail sings slow, to a tune of delight,
While fireflies dance, bringing glow to the night.
Each creature here, with a story to share,
In this canopy world, joy fills the air.

A bear joins in, juggling berries with glee,
He trips on a root, oh what a sight to see!
The leaves shout a laugh, shaking with mirth,
In the boughs of the trees, there's endless rebirth.

A Symphony of Nature's Embrace

The wind strums the branches, a playful refrain,
As crickets chirp laughter, a musical gain.
The squirrels conduct as the grasshoppers play,
In this orchestra of laughter, they dance all day.

A frog takes the stage with a jump and a croak,
While the turtles just chuckle, they're not in the joke.
Each leaf flutters gently, keeping time with the beat,
As twinkling stars join, oh what a treat!

The show gets bizarre as a fox brings a flute,
While ladybugs sway in their charming suit.
The harmony swells amidst merriment bright,
In this nature's concert, nothing feels tight.

The nightfall approaches, the fireflies glow,
The laughter just echoes, and rambunctious flow.
In this whimsical jam, with friends all around,
In the heart of the woods, joy's truly profound.

The Shelter of Connectivity

Gathered beneath, a motley crew,
Where chatter and giggles fill the view.
A beaver tells tales of rivers wide,
While a fox shares secrets with deer nearby.

A hedgehog pricks his spines with pride,
As ducks quack loud, "Oh, let's take a ride!"
The laughter bounces off the trunk so stout,
In this quirky gathering, there's never a doubt.

Old tortoise fumbles with his phone,
He snaps all the selfies, not wanting to moan.
The memories made in this playful clutch,
In a sprawling green home, they share so much.

And as the sun dips, casting shadows long,
They sing silly songs, all together strong.
Under this canopy of joy and delight,
Their bonds grow deeper, into the night.

Whispered Secrets in Rustling Leaves

In the shade where squirrels dance,
The gossip flows, a silly prance.
Acorns drop like secret notes,
While crickets sing, the laughter floats.

A pigeon struts with such great flair,
Wearing shades like he don't care.
While bees hum tunes, they buzz around,
In this green theatre, joy is found.

Chirping birds join in the fun,
Playing hide and seek, just run!
A frog leaps high without a doubt,
A belly flop, we scream and shout.

The wind tells tales of summer's glow,
Of silly pranks we've come to know.
As leaves chuckle with the breeze,
The day is bright, we laugh with ease.

The Gathering of Sunlit Souls

A meeting place where shadows play,
With sunbeams having quite a say.
The daisies gossip, quite refined,
While butterflies jump, all intertwined.

A worm in glasses reads the lore,
While ants parade on a tiny tour.
"Whose turn to dance?" a beetle seeks,
And all the blooms nod, using beaks.

The grass tickles toes, we giggle loud,
As daisies form a laughing crowd.
The world feels light, a joyful fling,
As petals sway to the song we sing.

With nectar drinks and cake of pine,
We raise a toast beneath the vine.
With hearts aglow, we share the cheer,
For every critter brings good beer.

Fables Amongst the Leaves

In a glade where tales are spun,
Fables dance beneath the sun.
A spider spins a web of yarn,
While chipmunks plot and laugh, no harm.

A tale of frogs with noble goals,
Who leap and dream and steal our scrolls.
The wise old owl hoots with delight,
As funny fables take their flight.

An exaggerated tale of might,
Where grasshoppers wear capes so bright.
With every chirp, a giggle flows,
As rabbits plot their cheeky shows.

So gather 'round, let stories roll,
Where laughter echoes, fills the soul.
With every leaf a secret told,
In this realm, we watch the bold.

Meditations Under the Branches

In a shady nook, we sit and muse,
Thoughtful ponderings, giggles fuse.
The branches sway, invite the fun,
As thoughts turn silly, one by one.

A snail makes plans for a grand race,
With a lazy smile upon its face.
While shadows stretch, they poke and tease,
As light and laughter swirl like breeze.

A squirrel's pondering deep life goals,
While hiding acorns over holes.
"Why gather nuts?" a wise worm checks,
"I'd rather feast on leafy specs!"

As giggles echo through the air,
The world escapes, we lose our care.
In this odd circle, joy is found,
With every chuckle, love abounds.

Reflections in the Shaded Grove

In the shade where squirrels dance,
And acorns drop like chance,
I found a hat upon the ground,
It looked like something quite profound.

A crow cawed loud, a raucous sound,
While grasshoppers leaped all around,
I shrugged and put that hat on straight,
Now I'm the king—what is my fate?

The Embrace of Timeworn Branches

Old branches bend with tales to tell,
Of picnics gone awry, and how they fell,
A raccoon munches on a slice of pie,
While giggling squirrels keep passing by.

The wind whispers secrets, quirky and bright,
As I climb up for a bird's-eye sight,
But lo and behold, my pants give way,
And now I'm stuck—what a lovely display!

Dreams Weaved in the Canopy

Swinging high on a rope so crude,
I dream of lunch—my favorite food,
But then I land in a pile of leaves,
With acorns sticking, oh how it weaves!

The chipmunks laugh and gather round,
In their nuts-and-seeds shrouded mound,
They chuckle softly at my plight,
As I sip my juice, green, and spiked!

A Refuge from Life's Storms

A rainy day, I sought a spot,
Where puddles form and worries rot,
But found a frog that took my seat,
And croaked with glee—what a fun feat!

With lightning flash and thunder loud,
The tree stood firm, a quiet crowd,
And I, soaked through, began to grin,
For frogs are champions, let the fun begin!

The Embrace of Earth and Sky

In a cozy nook, squirrels play,
Chasing tails in a wild ballet.
Birds gossip high, in a jestful spree,
While settling down for a brunch of brie.

With acorns tossed like daily news,
Frogs croak rhymes in their funny shoes.
The sun winks down with a cheeky glow,
As ants form lines for the beetle show.

Grass tickles toes, a friendly tease,
A hedgehog rolls by, searching for cheese.
The breeze carries laughter all around,
In this haven where joy knows no bound.

So gather 'round, let's laugh and sing,
For nature's stage is a comical thing.
In this wild world, the zany's the norm,
Where every creature performs in warm.

Forest Echoes of Timelessness

Time stands still where the tall ones sway,
Whispering secrets in a lighthearted way.
Bunnies hop like they're in a race,
While a turtle grins, no need for haste.

Twigs crack underfoot, a playful sound,
The raccoon laughs, always looking round.
With every rustle, a giggle erupts,
In this woodland where humor erupts.

The willows dance like they've lost their mind,
And the frogs croon songs that are one of a kind.
An owl calls, "Who's there?" with a grin,
While mice share tales of cheese and kin.

Time lingers long, filled with delight,
In this realm where all's merry and bright.
Nature's laughter, a timeless decree,
Echoes through branches, wild and free.

Conversations Among the Bark

The tree trunks chat about the weather,
Swapping stories, roots deep as leather.
Branches quip with a twist of glee,
Leaves nod along, as if to agree.

A lazy worm winds through the chat,
Catching gossip while sprawled out flat.
"I once saw a bird steal a pie!"
"Oh really?" says the bark, "You lie!"

A woodpecker drums a silly beat,
As the forest joins in on this meme treat.
Squirrels jest, "Watch your acorn stash,"
In the banter, they dash with a flash.

Each tree has tales both tall and wide,
Of adventures taken on nature's ride.
In the bark's embrace, all laughter sparks,
Creating joy in these wooded parks.

Epiphanies in the Rustling Leaves

The leaves gossip beneath the bright sun,
Sharing laughter, life can be so fun.
"Did you hear what that crow did today?"
"Oh, spill the tea! I'm all ears, hey!"

A rabbit munches, rolling his eyes,
At silly tales spun from mystery skies.
The grass sways along in a dance so grand,
While butterflies flit, all part of the band.

Winds whisper jokes from the clouds above,
As they sway in rhythm, a breezy love.
"Who's the champion of tree-climbing game?"
"Definitely not the one with the name!"

Laughter spills over as daylight wanes,
Nature's comedians in their domains.
In rustling leaves, the joy persists,
Where humor and life can't be missed.

Beneath the Branches of Time's Keeper

In a shade where giggles bloom,
Squirrels dance, making room.
Ticklish leaves brush the ground,
As old tales dance all around.

The ancient trunk, a throne of jest,
Draws in friends for a merry fest.
Laughter echoes, birds take flight,
In the soft, dappled light.

A raccoon dons a tiny hat,
Swaggers by, a cheeky brat.
With a wink and a cheeky grin,
Join the fun, come jump in!

The acorns drop like silly bombs,
Cheerful chaos, playful qualms.
Nature's humor blooms with ease,
Under this giant, feel the breeze.

Where Roots Interlace with History

Where knobby roots play and twist,
Past secrets sigh, they can't resist.
A garden gnome, bright and spry,
Mischief twinkles in his eye.

The old tree chuckles with delight,
As shadows dance in the fading light.
Caterpillars groan 'this is rough',
While ants just shrug, 'we're tough enough!'

A fox strolls by with a jaunty flair,
Searching for treats he can't quite share.
The history here is full of cheer,
With each squirrel's tale, the past feels near.

Beneath the roots, a party brews,
Dancing shoes on fuzzy snooze.
So come along, and lose your cares,
Join the laughter that fills the air.

The Sanctuary of the Silent Watcher

A wise old face with barky frown,
Watches kids run up and down.
"Don't climb too high!" he seems to say,
As they swing and laugh, at play.

Beneath his gaze, the jokes take flight,
A pair of squirrels start a fight.
"Did you steal my acorn stash?"
"Not me! I'm just here to dash!"

The laughter swells, their antics grand,
A toad leaps by, a tiny band.
"Join our show!" the critters shout,
In this woods, there's never doubt.

The ancient tree, with roots so deep,
Keeps all laughter, our secrets to keep.
In his shade, the world feels light,
With every chuckle, hearts take flight.

Murmurs in the Underbrush

Whispers rustle through the green,
Chirps of joy, what a scene!
Beneath the ferns, a giggle sighs,
As tiny bugs play peek-a-boo wise.

A hedgehog rolls, then stops to sneeze,
While rabbits hold a game, if you please.
"Don't eat the daisies!" was the call,
But nibbling here brings smiles for all.

Gnomes gossip in the soft, wet ground,
As the breeze dances all around.
"Did you hear that? This spot's the best!
The humor here won't let you rest!"

Amidst the rustle, a song appears,
Tickly sounds tickle our ears.
In the underbrush, let laughs grow vast,
Where joys are simple, and smiles last.

The Stillness of Nature's Heart

In the shade of a giant tree,
Squirrels plot their grand spree.
Acorns fly with joyous glee,
As birds laugh in harmony.

A turtle takes a brisk stroll,
While ants prepare a food bowl.
The breeze whispers as they roll,
Nature hosts a silly carnival.

The fox trots by in a cool hat,
Winking at a fuzzy brat.
The sun shines brightly, how 'bout that?
This woodland's quite the chatty mat!

With a wink and a playful chase,
Every critter finds their place.
The stillness breaks into a race,
In this leafy, lively space.

Sanctuary of Swaying Branches

In the branches, a dance unfolds,
Where shadows play tricks, truth be told.
A raccoon juggles breakfast rolls,
While a wise owl shares fun-filled folds.

Leaves rustle, announcing the show,
Grasshoppers leap to steal the glow.
A squirrel's acrobatics grow,
As laughter echoes, high and low.

Beneath the boughs, the frogs reply,
With croaks and quacks, oh my, oh my!
The wind joins in, a gentle sigh,
In this sanctuary where spirits fly.

Life's a picnic, snacks abound,
In this funny patch of ground.
Where branches playfully confound,
Nature's joy is all around.

Rustling Tales of the Woodland Spirits

In twilight's glow, whispers weave,
Tree spirits gather, night to perceive.
A gnome with a loaf gave a big heave,
As fairies plotted tricks up their sleeve.

The bushes chuckled, a private joke,
While hedgehogs conspire, poky folks.
"Why don't trees play cards?" one said, "They're oaks!"
Nature's laughter, a chorus of croaks.

Bats flit about in an aerial race,
Hiding from the light, they embrace space.
A raccoon in a mask takes his place,
While the moon giggles, lighting the place.

Rustling tales swirl in the air,
In the night, magic everywhere.
Nature's spirits with joy to share,
In laughter's glow, they dance and care.

The Peace Found in Nature's Arms

In a patch of grass so lush and bright,
A frog croaks tunes till the moon's light.
Crickets chirp, oh what a sight!
Nature calls, and all takes flight.

Buzzing bees in a playful spree,
Skipping flowers, oh what glee!
While ladybugs sip green tea,
Chasing echoes, fancy-free.

A hedgehog dons a tiny coat,
The forest giggles at his boat.
With every turn, giggles float,
In nature's arms, we're all a goat.

The peace here comes with a jest,
As nature laughs, we feel so blessed.
In the woods, humor is the best,
Join in the fun, forget the rest.

Beneath the Knotted Canopy

Squirrels throw acorns with glee,
Chatting gossip, not a care,
While birds chirp tales, oh so free,
In this tree, life's a fair.

Sunbeams dance through the leaves,
As branches play hide and seek,
Nature's laughter, how it weaves,
With whispers that gently peek.

A raccoon dons a leafy crown,
Pretending to be the king,
Among the roots, no hint of frown,
And the breeze begins to sing.

All around, joy takes its flight,
A tiny owl falls in a swoon,
His feathered friends take to the height,
As they gossip under the moon.

Ceremonies of Light and Leaf

A sunny spot where shadows play,
Ants march in their quirky lines,
Dancing leaves join in the fray,
While nature's humor brightly shines.

A squirrel twirls like it's unsure,
Spinning tales of daring feats,
As butterflies float, pure allure,
Drawing giggles from little beats.

The sun sneezes, a warm delight,
Leaves flutter down, what a show!
A rabbit hops in sheer delight,
Wearing clovers, don't you know?

With each breeze, a chuckle's found,
Nature's stand-up, so sublime,
Beneath the green and earthy ground,
Laughter echoes through all time.

Heartbeats in the Forest's Core

A woodland pulse, so full of cheer,
With chattering friends on a branch,
A caterpillar holds its beer,
While ants plot the next big ranch.

Mushrooms wear tiny top hats,
As crickets serenade the night,
Whiskers twitch on curious cats,
While fireflies flaunt their bright light.

A hedgehog rolls with perfect flair,
Claiming victory, what a scene,
As rabbits cheer, "How's the hair?"
In the green, where laughter's keen.

Nature's heartbeat, playful leaps,
A symphony of light and sound,
In every corner, laughter seeps,
In this core, joy is profound.

The Embrace of Nature's Ancients

Gnarled limbs stretch out, arms wide,
Golden laughs echo through time,
Birds gossip as they glide,
In this ancient leafy rhyme.

Knobby roots with tales to tell,
Of critters bold and storms endured,
In the shade, all is swell,
A comedy of life assured.

Chipmunks giggle as they race,
Competing for the biggest nut,
Each acorn's more than just a chase,
It's a treasure that they strut.

Beneath the wise and leafy lore,
Every breeze brings silly cheer,
In this embrace, we laugh and explore,
Nature's jesters, loud and clear.

Chasing Dreams Beneath the Canopy

Squirrels in suits are making a scene,
Bouncing about, they act like a queen.
Chasing their tails in a dizzying dance,
Who knew a tree could harbor such prance?

Birds chime in with their comedic tune,
Mocking the cats who think they're immune.
Laughter erupts as branches sway wide,
In this leafy world, there's nowhere to hide.

The sun peeks through like a curious guest,
Tickling the leaves, they chuckle and jest.
If only the world could see this ballet,
A circus of laughter, come join in the play!

So grab your lunch, your friends, and your cheer,
Let's picnic below without any fear.
For dreams are chasing each other like kids,
In the grand old tree that's savvy and mid.

Suspended in Nature's Grasp

Swinging from branches like kites in the sky,
We twirl and we turn, oh my, oh my!
The laughter of leaves whispers sweetly to us,
As we stumble and tumble, causing a fuss.

A raccoon peeked in, wearing a hat,
He winked and he slipped, what a sight that cat!
Joined by a frog who's stuck in a glance,
Together they work to conjure a dance.

Nature's circus on a sunbeam so bright,
We stand on our heads, what a curious sight!
Juggling the moments of joy and of glee,
With acorns and giggles, just you wait and see!

So stretch out your limbs and feel the embrace,
Let the winds tickle you, just join in the race.
For life is a jest that we've come here to claim,
In this timeless realm of laughter and fame.

Intimacy among the Green Giants

Whispers among leaves, secrets abound,
Sap in the air, our laughter profound.
Ants marching proudly in a tiny parade,
They salute with gusto, 'We won't be dismayed!'

A worm tells a joke, and the grass starts to sway,
The daisies all giggle, 'What a fine day!'
With fireflies blinking, they join in our cheer,
Creating a symphony for all who draw near.

Mushrooms act silly with caps on their heads,
Pretending to nod as they lie in their beds.
A playful rabbit hops in with a grin,
Shouting, 'Who's ready for some hide-and-seek spin?'

Beneath all that green, oh, what fun we find,
A mishmash of craziness, perfectly timed.
So laugh with the trees, let your spirit be free,
In this world full of whimsy, come climb with me!

Enchantment at the Tree's Heart

At the roots of spirits, the magic is real,
Fairies drink lemonade, spinning wheels with zeal.
With petals as hats and laughter in their eyes,
They churn up the mischief beneath painted skies.

A turtle in slippers, he shuffles along,
As crickets compose a peculiar song.
The joy of the grass tickles feet in delight,
While children join in for a hop and a flight.

Giggling pinecones bounce out of their shells,
Sharing stories and secrets like whimsical spells.
What joy unfolds at this enchanted spree,
With giggles and glee, oh, come dance with me!

So skip to the heart of this jovial place,
Where silliness thrives and laughter finds space.
For magic is real in the fun that we share,
At the trunk of a wonder, it's all in the air!

In the Shade of Wisdom's Boughs

Sitting snug with my sandwich,
A squirrel steals my chip!
He winks, and I can't help but giggle,
As I contemplate my next trip.

The branches sway, a gentle tease,
While bees hum, buzzing in tune.
Who knew nature held a comedy,
And laughter would make me immune?

My thoughts drift like leaves in the breeze,
Should I give a nut or just glare?
The cheeky little scamp keeps asking,
If I've got shares in acorn fare!

Under such shelter, I plot my chance,
To reclaim my lost salted prize.
But the playful critter takes a stance,
And dances away with sparkling eyes.

A Respite Amongst the Flora

Here I sit on nature's throne,
Surrounded by flowers' cheer.
A gopher pops his head, quite bold,
Squeaking tales of gardening fear.

The daisies nod in gentle mirth,
As I share secrets with the dandelions.
They all laugh when I confess,
I forget my plants need daily alignments!

A butterfly flutters with a wink,
Saying, 'Your pruning skills need work!'
I throw my hands up, jesting,
With blooms concealing my trademark smirk.

The sun dips low, the day rolls on,
Nature's laughter echoes loud.
In this garden of chuckles spun,
I wear my sunshine like a proud crown.

Penumbra of Heartfelt Encounters

In shadow's embrace, I greet my friend,
A raccoon with tricks up his sleeve.
He points to my snack with an eager grin,
I guess sharing's what I must believe!

Laughing together, we plot our feast,
As fireflies join our jolly parade.
Who knew evenings could bring such fun?
With antics crafted, the sunset's made!

The moon joins in—now that's a treat!
Winking at us from above.
We dance in whispers, so sweetly discreet,
In nature's embrace, we forge our love.

So here we'll remain, both wild and free,
Amid laughter and snacks, we draw near.
In shadows and light, we're just as we be,
A pair of goofballs—let's toast with cheer!

Harmony of Roots and Sky

Beneath the boughs, it's time to play,
With giggles that echo all around.
The ants march by in a silly line,
I'm their queen, or so I found!

Sunbeams peek, a spotlight high,
As I tell tales of my daring quests.
The wind listens in with a playful sigh,
Ready to join in as my guest.

Birds serenade from treetop heights,
While I attempt to sing along.
Their chirps don't mind if I mess it up,
For off-key notes can't do me wrong!

With laughter, we dance through the day,
In harmony with roots, both steady and sly.
Nature's joy brings a smile to stay,
As we giggle beneath the endless sky!

A Quiet Communion with Nature

A squirrel stole my sandwich, oh dear,
I chased it round, but it disappeared!
The leaves giggled down, what a sight!
Nature's sense of humor is always bright.

Beneath the branches, shadows dance,
I watched a worm do a little prance.
He slipped and slid on a leaf so slick,
Who knew worms had such a funny trick?

Bees buzzed near, with a raucous hum,
Their buzzing rhythm, a silly drum.
Flowers chuckled in the gentle breeze,
Nature's laughter puts my mind at ease.

A frog leaped by with a mighty croak,
"Excuse me, sir!" he seemed to joke.
In the wild, it's all a comic play,
A quiet laugh in a mossy display.

A Reverie at the Tree's Base

Laying back, I spotted a face,
A cloud that wore a funny grace.
It seemed to giggle as it floated by,
I chuckled aloud, oh me, oh my!

Ants marched on, a bustling line,
In tiny uniforms, they looked divine.
But one slipped down, slipped right on by,
His comrades laughed with a playful cry.

The trees swayed with a playful wink,
I wondered what they might think.
A rustling joke from branch to ground,
In this serene spot, laughter's found.

With a rustle and a cheer, the wind did play,
Brushing leaves in a silly way.
Here at the base, where life takes a pause,
Nature's humor finds its cause.

The Gathering Place of the Wanderer

Travelers come with stories to share,
Beneath the boughs, they burst at the air.
One told of ducks that danced in a line,
Quacking a tune, oh what a sign!

A rollicking fox joined in the fun,
His wiggly tail was second to none.
He told a tale of a mischievous hare,
Who painted the fence, just to scare!

Around this spot, tales grow long,
With laughter echoing like a sweet song.
A gathering place for all who dare,
To pause and share, to breathe the air.

Even a crow with a glittery beak,
Cawed a punchline, oh what a cheek!
With humor stitched into every heart,
Together in laughter, we play our part.

Whispers Shared by Gentle Breezes

The wind whistled secrets, soft and sly,
Tickling tufts of grass nearby.
I heard it snicker, low and sweet,
As dandelions danced on little feet.

"Where's the party?" a sparrow chirped,
He flapped and flittered, his humor perked.
They plotted 'round a sleepy cat,
Dreaming of fish, now how about that?

Around the trunk, a rabbit peeked,
With a carrot hat—how unique!
He winked and twitched, say what a sight,
Nature's fashion show—quite a delight!

When the night falls, stars start their jokes,
With twinkling laughs that dance like folks.
In breezes shared and whispers sweet,
Nature's humor can't be beat!

Reflections in Nature's Embrace

A squirrel prances, oh so bold,
Munching acorns, stories told.
The bugs all chuckle, they aim to tease,
As branches sway in the playful breeze.

A rabbit hops with a lopsided grin,
Singing songs to coax a win.
Leaves gossip softly, whispers of cheer,
While ants parade, they have no fear.

The shadows dance on the forest floor,
Beneath the branches, who could ask for more?
Nature's stage, a comedic affair,
With critters prancing, without a care.

So here we laugh amidst green delight,
As evening falls, and day turns to night.
A cheerful place, with humor at hand,
In this wild world, we all take a stand.

A Canvas of Shade and Light

On a sunny day, the sun takes flight,
Painting shadows, with humor so bright.
A hound sprawls out, claiming his throne,
While a wily fox sneaks off with a bone.

Bees buzz around, sharing their tales,
Of far-off flowers and wind-blown gales.
With each flip of a leaf and flutter of wing,
Laughter rises, it's nature's spring.

Children giggle, chasing their dreams,
Reckless and wild, bursting at seams.
While the elder trees chuckle in jest,
Unfurling their branches, nature's best.

So let's play on, in this joyous scene,
Where laughter and light create a keen sheen.
In this canvas, we dance and roam,
Forever entwined, in nature's home.

Harmony in Gnarled Serenity

The old tree leans, with a twist and a bend,
In its gnarled embrace, all troubles mend.
A parade of critters, each with a quirk,
To scamper and dash, all busy at work.

A woodpecker knocks, a tap-tap-tap,
While a curious fellow tries to take a nap.
The branches sway in a ticklish dance,
As sunlight streams in, igniting romance.

Chirps and chirrups fill the air,
A chorus of creatures, quite the affair.
In this awkward harmony, joy finds a way,
As laughter sprouts, brightening the day.

So gather around, let the giggles resound,
In the crook of the branches, pure joy can be found.
With every breeze, we revel anew,
In this silly jangle, life's funny hue.

Tendrils of Memory in the Shade

Beneath lush green, in twilight glow,
Where stories linger, they ebb and flow.
A family of ducks waddle in line,
Quacking in rhythm, oh-so-divine.

A lazy cat sprawls, sunlight her guide,
While butterflies join in a whimsical ride.
The old tree winks, from a thousand years,
As laughter erupts, chasing away fears.

Footprints of fun scatter the ground,
In shadows and whispers, memories abound.
A picnic spread out, with treats to share,
In this silly place, we breathe the fresh air.

So let the giggles twine in the leaves,
With every rustle, the heart believes.
In this tale of shade, our spirits gleam,
Where laughter flourishes, in nature's dream.

www.ingramcontent.com/pod-product-compliance
Lightning Source LLC
Chambersburg PA
CBHW051634160426
43209CB00004B/648